D0884423

**PRESIDENTS**

# FRANKLIN D. ROOSEVELT

## A MyReportLinks.com Book

Ron Knapp

MyReportLinks.com Books
an imprint of
 **Enslow Publishers, Inc.**
Box 398, 40 Industrial Road
Berkeley Heights, NJ 07922
USA

MyReportLinks.com Books, an imprint of Enslow Publishers, Inc.

Copyright © 2002 by Enslow Publishers, Inc.

All rights reserved.

No part of this book may be reproduced by any means
without the written permission of the publisher.

**Library of Congress Cataloging-in-Publication Data**


Knapp, Ron.
   Franklin D. Roosevelt : A MyReportLinks.com Book / Ron Knapp.
      p. cm. — (Presidents)
   Includes bibliographical references and index.
   Summary: Traces the life of the only president to be elected four times. Includes
Internet Links to Web sites, source documents, and photographs related to Franklin
Delano Roosevelt.
   ISBN 0-7660-5009-2
   1.  Roosevelt, Franklin D. (Franklin Delano), 1882–1945—Juvenile literature. 2.
Presidents—United States—Biography—Juvenile literature. [1. Roosevelt, Franklin D.
(Franklin Delano), 1882–1945. 2. Presidents.]  I. Title. II. Series.

   E807 .K63 2002
   973.917'092—dc21
   [B]

                                                                            2001004264



Printed in the United States of America

10 9 8 7 6 5 4 3 2 1

**To Our Readers:** We have done our best to make sure all Internet addresses in this book
were active and appropriate when we went to press. However, the author and the Publisher
have no control over, and assume no liability for, the material available on those Internet
sites or on other Web sites they may link to. The Publisher will try to keep the Report Links
that back up this book up to date on our Web site for three years from the book's
first publication date. Any comments or suggestions can be sent by e-mail to
comments@myreportlinks.com or to the address on the back cover.

**Photo Credits:** © Corel Corporation, pp. 1 (background), 3; Courtesy of
Campobello Park Commission, p. 24; Courtesy of *Dictionary of American
Portraits*, Dover Publications, Inc., © 1967, p. 28; Courtesy of FDR Library, pp.
11, 15, 19, 23, 33, 40, 42, 44; Courtesy of Franklin & Eleanor Roosevelt
Institute, p. 16; Courtesy of National Park Service, p. 14; Courtesy of New Deal
Network, pp. 27, 35; Courtesy of Tennessee Valley Authority, p. 31; Courtesy of
The American Experience, p. 38; Courtesy of U.S Naval Historical Center, p. 39;
Library of Congress, pp. 1, 20.

**Cover Photos:** © Corel Corporation (background); Franklin D. Roosevelt Library.

# Contents

**Report Links** . . . . . . . . . . . . . . . . . . . . . . . . . . **4**

**Highlights** . . . . . . . . . . . . . . . . . . . . . . . . . . . . **10**

**1** **"Nothing to Fear," 1932** . . . . . . . . . . . . . . **11**

**2** **Early Life, 1880–1910** . . . . . . . . . . . . . . . . . **14**

**3** **Setbacks and Successes,**
    **1913–1932** . . . . . . . . . . . . . . . . . . . . . . . . **22**

**4** **The New Deal and Early Presidency,**
    **1933–1940** . . . . . . . . . . . . . . . . . . . . . . . . **30**

**5** **World War II to the End,**
    **1940–1945** . . . . . . . . . . . . . . . . . . . . . . . . **37**

**Chapter Notes** . . . . . . . . . . . . . . . . . . . . . . . . **45**

**Further Reading** . . . . . . . . . . . . . . . . . . . . . . **47**

**Index** . . . . . . . . . . . . . . . . . . . . . . . . . . . . . . . **48**

# MyReportLinks.com Books
## Great Books, Great Links, Great for Research!

MyReportLinks.com Books present the information you need to learn about your report subject. In addition, they show you where to go on the Internet for more information. The pre-evaluated Report Links, listed on **www.myreportlinks.com**, save hours of research time and link to dozens—even hundreds—of Web sites, source documents, and photos related to your report topic.

**To Our Readers:**
Each Report Link has been reviewed by our editors, who will work hard to keep only active and appropriate Internet addresses in our books and up to date on our Web site. However, the author and the Publisher have no control over, and assume no liability for, the material available on those Internet sites, or on other Web sites they may link to.

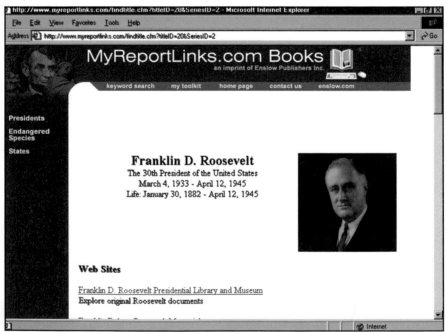

**Access:**
The Publisher will try to keep the Report Links that back up this book up to date on our Web site for three years from the book's first publication date. Please enter **PRO1338** if asked for a password.

## Report Links

 The Internet sites described below can be accessed at
**http://www.myreportlinks.com**

*EDITOR'S CHOICE

## ▶ Franklin D. Roosevelt Library & Digital Archives

The Franklin D. Roosevelt Library & Digital Archives contains thirteen
thousand digitalized documents and photographs. You will also find
links to information about the Great Depression, and the biographies
of Franklin and Eleanor Roosevelt.

Link to this Internet site from http://www.myreportlinks.com

*EDITOR'S CHOICE

## ▶ Franklin Delano Roosevelt Memorial

This site describes the four rooms of the Franklin Delano
Roosevelt Memorial. Each room explores one of the four terms
served by Roosevelt.

Link to this Internet site from http://www.myreportlinks.com

*EDITOR'S CHOICE

## ▶ Franklin & Eleanor Roosevelt Institute

Franklin & Eleanor Roosevelt Institute provides biographies
on Franklin and Eleanor Roosevelt. You can also explore a time line
of FDR's life, photographs, numerous speeches, and a press kit.

Link to this Internet site from http://www.myreportlinks.com

*EDITOR'S CHOICE

## ▶ Franklin D. Roosevelt

This site contains a time line documenting important events in
Franklin D. Roosevelt's life including the Great Depression and World
War II. You will also find an audio excerpt from Roosevelt's 1941
address to Congress.

Link to this Internet site from http://www.myreportlinks.com

*EDITOR'S CHOICE

## ▶ The American Presidency: Franklin D. Roosevelt

Grolier provides a comprehensive biography of the only president to be
elected to four consecutive terms. This site contains links to each of
Roosevelt's inaugural addresses, and quick facts about his life.

Link to this Internet site from http://www.myreportlinks.com

*EDITOR'S CHOICE

## ▶ The Presidents: FDR

This PBS site traces Franklin D. Roosevelt's political career. Here you
will learn of Roosevelt's presidential policies that transformed the
presidency and government.

Link to this Internet site from http://www.myreportlinks.com

The Internet sites described below can be accessed at
**http://www.myreportlinks.com**

▶ **About TVA: A Short History of TVA: From the New Deal to a New Century**

This site contains the history of the Tennessee Valley Authority Act, a New Deal initiative. The TVA provided many unemployed people with jobs, and dramatically improved the conditions of farms in the Tennessee Valley.

Link to this Internet site from http://www.myreportlinks.com

▶ **The American Presidency: Eleanor Roosevelt**

Grolier's biography of Eleanor Roosevelt reveals the years she devoted to achieving social change. Learn how Eleanor's unprecedented actions in the White House and in her life led her to be an important political figure in her own right.

Link to this Internet site from http://www.myreportlinks.com

▶ **Character above All: Franklin D. Roosevelt**

At this site you can read an excerpt from an essay which explores the character of Franklin D. Roosevelt. It shows that confidence in himself, and approval from the American people, were very important to Roosevelt.

Link to this Internet site from http://www.myreportlinks.com

▶ **Eleanor Roosevelt 1884–1962**

This biography explores the political life of Eleanor Roosevelt and what it was like to be a politically active woman in the twentieth century.

Link to this Internet site from http://www.myreportlinks.com

▶ **Einstein to Roosevelt, August 2, 1939**

This site holds a letter written to Franklin D. Roosevelt from Albert Einstein. The letter concerns the possibility of Germany building an atomic bomb.

Link to this Internet site from http://www.myreportlinks.com

▶ **Fireside Chats of Franklin D. Roosevelt**

At this Web site you will find a collection of the famous radio addresses delivered by Franklin Delano Roosevelt from 1933 through 1944.

Link to this Internet site from http://www.myreportlinks.com

## Report Links

 The Internet sites described below can be accessed at
**http://www.myreportlinks.com**

▶ **Franklin Delano Roosevelt**
This Web site provides facts and figures on Franklin Delano Roosevelt.
Here you will find links to Roosevelt's election results, cabinet
members, historical documents, and Internet biographies.

Link to this Internet site from http://www.myreportlinks.com

▶ **Franklin Delano Roosevelt**
This Web site provides a comprehensive biography of Franklin D.
Roosevelt. Learn about his life before and during his presidency, and
the impact he had on the American people and the federal government.

Link to this Internet site from http://www.myreportlinks.com

▶ **Franklin Delano Roosevelt (1882–1945)**
This online archive contains all of Franklin D. Roosevelt's Inaugural
Addresses, State of the Union messages, and the Pearl Harbor speech.
You will also find links to FDR's fireside chats.

Link to this Internet site from http://www.myreportlinks.com

▶ **Franklin D. Roosevelt**
Grolier's Online World War II Commemoration contains many links to
information on World War II, including a brief history of the war,
biographies, films, photographs, a test, and links to other resources.

Link to this Internet site from http://www.myreportlinks.com

▶ **Franklin D. Roosevelt (1882–1945)**
By navigating through this site you will find the portrait of Franklin D.
Roosevelt that hangs in the National Portrait Gallery. Read a brief
profile of FDR and many other presidents.

Link to this Internet site from http://www.myreportlinks.com

▶ **Great Depression And World War II, 1929–1945**
This site explores the ways in which Franklin D. Roosevelt's presidency
improved the lives of American's struggling through the depression, and
how he redefined the role of federal government.

Link to this Internet site from http://www.myreportlinks.com

The Internet sites described below can be accessed at
**http://www.myreportlinks.com**

### Home of Franklin D. Roosevelt
Learn about Franklin D. Roosevelt's family, personal life, and rise to presidency at this National Park Service site.

Link to this Internet site from http://www.myreportlinks.com

### A New Deal for the Arts
This site describes how New Deal programs supported the Arts for eleven years. Featured at this site are paintings and photographs documenting American life.

Link to this Internet site from http://www.myreportlinks.com

### New Deal Cultural Programs: Experiments in Cultural Democracy
This site explores the ways in which the New Deal supported the arts. Read descriptions of the cultural programs under the New Deal which supported visual art, music, theater, and literature.

Link to this Internet site from http://www.myreportlinks.com

### New Deal Network
The New Deal Network is a teaching and resource tool where you can explore a vast number of documents, photographs, and other resources related to the New Deal era.

Link to this Internet site from http://www.myreportlinks.com

### Presidential Elections 1896–1996
The *New York Times* on the Web Learning Network summarizes Franklin D. Roosevelt's 1940 and 1944 elections. Read historic articles from 1941 to 1945.

Link to this Internet site from http://www.myreportlinks.com

### The Roosevelt Campobello International Park Commission
Roosevelt Campobello International Park Commission was established in 1964 through an agreement between President Lyndon B. Johnson and Canadian Prime Minister Lester B. Pearson. This park commemorates the friendship between the United States and Canada.

Link to this Internet site from http://www.myreportlinks.com

## Report Links

The Internet sites described below can be accessed at
**http://www.myreportlinks.com**

### ▶Roosevelt asks Congress to Declare War
This site contains numerous photographs and posters documenting
the history of the World War II. Browse through images of the Pearl
Harbor attack, Winston Churchill, Franklin Roosevelt, and World
War II battles.

Link to this Internet site from http://www.myreportlinks.com

### ▶Roosevelt, Franklin Delano
DiscoverySchool.com provides a biography that outlines FDR's
life from early childhood through his presidency. View tables with
important dates in Roosevelt's life, quotations, and highlights of
his administration.

Link to this Internet site from http://www.myreportlinks.com

### ▶Time 100: Franklin Delano Roosevelt
Time.com profiles Franklin D. Roosevelt along with nineteen other
influential leaders and revolutionaries. Learn how FDR changed the
American way of life.

Link to this Internet site from http://www.myreportlinks.com

### ▶USS *Arizona* Memorial Fund
The Pearl Harbor memorial site provides a history of the Pearl Harbor
attack along with photographs documenting the event.

Link to this Internet site from http://www.myreportlinks.com

### ▶The White House: Anna Eleanor Roosevelt
The official White House Web site holds the biography of Anna
Eleanor Roosevelt. An influential woman of her generation, Eleanor
Roosevelt used her position as first lady to improve social conditions.

Link to this Internet site from http://www.myreportlinks.com

### ▶The White House: Franklin D. Roosevelt
The official White House Web site holds the biography of Franklin D.
Roosevelt. Learn how Roosevelt gave hope to a nation suffering
through the depression.

Link to this Internet site from http://www.myreportlinks.com

## Highlights

**1882**—*Jan. 30:* Born in Hyde Park, New York.

**1903**—Graduates from Harvard.

**1905**—*March 17:* Marries Eleanor Roosevelt.

**1907**—Passes the New York state bar exam, allowing him to practice law.

**1910**—Elected to New York state senate.

**1913–1920**—Serves as assistant secretary of the Navy.

**1920**—Unsuccessfully runs for vice president on a ticket with presidential candidate James Cox.

**1921**—Stricken with the disease polio.

**1928**—Elected governor of New York.

**1932**—Elected president of the United States over the former president, Herbert Hoover. John Nance Garner is Roosevelt's vice president.

**1933**—Launches the New Deal, a series of laws and regulations designed to jump-start the economy and help end the Great Depression.

—First president to engage in diplomatic relations with the Soviet Union.

**1936**—Reelected president over Alfred (Alf) M. Landon.

**1940**—Reelected president over Wendell Willkie. Henry Agard Wallace is Roosevelt's second vice president.

**1941**—*Dec. 7:* Japan invades United States military base at Pearl Harbor, Hawaii. The following day Roosevelt asks Congress for a declaration of war, and the United States formally enters World War II.

**1944**—Reelected to fourth term as president over Thomas E. Dewey. Harry Truman becomes Roosevelt's third vice president.

—*June 6:* Allied forces under General Eisenhower land in Normandy, France, in what became known as the D-Day invasion.

**1945**—*April 12:* Dies at his vacation home in Warm Springs, Georgia. Truman becomes president.

## Chapter 1

# "Nothing to Fear," 1932

**A**mericans in 1932 were living at a scary time. The country was almost out of money. Even many of the banks had no money left in their vaults. This period was known as the Great Depression.

Without enough cash, thousands of factories and businesses had to close. More than 15 million people were out of work. The lucky workers who still had jobs saw their

▲ This is a familiar scene from the Great Depression. Since many people lost their jobs and homes, they had to live in slums, like the one pictured here.

wages cut. Some teachers and other government workers had months of "payless paydays." They worked for nothing, hoping one day to be paid. Farm prices fell so low that it cost more to grow and harvest crops than farmers could earn from selling them.

Families with little or no money could not afford to make house payments. Millions of them lost their homes. More than two hundred thousand of the homeless were children. Of course, families with little or no money could not afford enough food, either. When one little girl was too hungry to do her schoolwork, her teacher told her to go home and get something to eat. "I can't," she said. "This is my sister's day to eat."[1] Another girl watched her brother play with his pet rabbit. "He thinks we aren't going to eat it," she whispered to a visitor, "but we are."[2] Other families had it even worse. Malnutrition was common, and some people starved.

Herbert Hoover was president during the early days of the Great Depression. He did not feel it was the government's responsibility to find homes for the homeless, jobs for the unemployed, or food for the hungry. Hoover felt that many people's problems could be solved if they simply worked harder. Still, people could not work harder when there were no jobs available. Hoover also believed it was the task of churches and private charities to take care of the poor.

Millions of Americans were desperate. Private charities and churches could not take care of all of them. Every day the situation grew worse. Worst of all, their own government did not even seem to care. Like American citizens then and today, Hoover favored small government, or little government involvement in people's lives.

Then along came Franklin D. Roosevelt (FDR), the governor of New York. When the Democratic Party nominated Roosevelt for president, he said, "I pledge you, I pledge myself to a New Deal for the American people."[3] He said it was time for the government to help its people. "The country demands bold, persistent experimentation."[4]

American voters liked his attitude. In the 1932 presidential election, Roosevelt beat Hoover in a landslide. When he became president on March 4, 1933, Roosevelt was confident: "This great nation will endure as it has endured, will revive and prosper . . ." he proclaimed. "The only thing we have to fear is fear itself."[5]

The nation cheered when he said, "Our greatest primary task is to put people to work." Over the next few months, dozens of plans poured out of the White House. Billions of dollars were spent feeding families, supporting banks and businesses, and creating jobs. Roosevelt knew that not all his ideas would work. "Take a method and try it," he told his advisors. "If it fails, try another. But above all, try something."[6]

Almost overnight the mood of the country changed. After hearing their confident president, Americans once again dared hope for better tomorrows. In his first week in the White House, these grateful Americans sent Roosevelt almost a million pieces of mail. Slowly, steadily, people went back to work. Businesses and factories reopened. Banks quit running out of money. The Great Depression began to ease.

For the next twelve years, Franklin Roosevelt's speeches and ideas changed the United States forever. Americans knew from his smile and his upturned chin that he loved what he was doing. "Wouldn't you be president if you could?" he once asked a visitor. "Wouldn't anybody?"[7]

# Early Life, 1880–1910

**F**ranklin Delano Roosevelt was a spoiled, but lonely little boy. His father, James, was a tall, thin man with long, bushy sideburns called muttonchops. The Roosevelts were so wealthy that James did not have to work. When he was not traveling, he spent his time at the family's mansion in Hyde Park, New York.

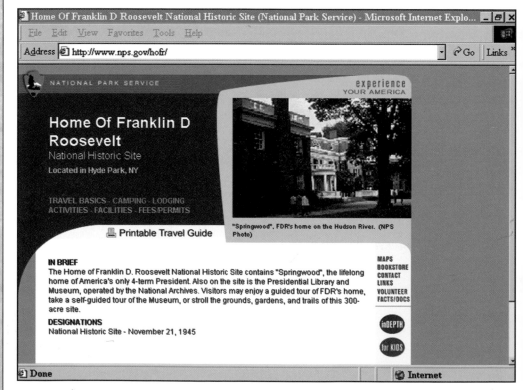

Located in Hyde Park, "Springfield" was the lifelong home of Franklin D. Roosevelt.

*As a young boy, Franklin spent a great deal of time with his father, engaging in various activities such as ice skating, playing tennis, and sailing.*

James Roosevelt was fifty-three years old when Franklin was born on January 30, 1882. His wife, Sara, was only twenty-six. Despite his age, Mr. Roosevelt was a very active man. He loved to ice-skate, play tennis, ride horses, and go sailing. Soon his little boy was at his side. Franklin was almost always with his parents. Very rarely was he allowed to play with other children. Instead of going to school, he had his own tutors at the mansion.

Sara Roosevelt devoted almost all her time and energy to raising her son. She made him follow a rigid daily schedule. There were definite times for eating, studying, playing, and sleeping. To keep the little boy happy, he was given just about everything he wanted. Franklin had a fluffy little puppy named Budgy. He also had a pony and a donkey. When he wanted a boat, his father let him borrow the family yacht. Soon he had a twenty-foot boat of his own. When he became interested in birds, his parents brought in experts to teach him how to mount and stuff them. Soon his collection was better than that of most museums. When he became interested in stamp collecting,

http://www.feri.org/fdr/images/fdr09.gif - Microsoft Internet Explorer

File  Edit  View  Favorites  Tools  Help

Address  http://www.feri.org/fdr/images/fdr09.gif                              Go   Links

Done                                                        Internet

▲ *Although the family had many servants and nurses, Sara Roosevelt was a very protective and devoted mother. She continued to play an active role in her son's life even after his marriage.*

his relatives sent him stamps from around the world. His collection became one of the most famous in the nation.

Almost every year, the Roosevelts spent several months touring Europe. Franklin spent more time visiting foreign buildings than he did playing with children his own age. When he was with other boys and girls, he did not have much fun because he was not sure how to act. He was more comfortable with adults. They thought the little boy with the golden curls was a sweet, well-behaved gentleman.

When Franklin was eight, his father suffered a severe heart attack. No longer could he play games or ride horses with his son. He spent his time resting. Franklin worried about his father. When Franklin cut his head, he made his mother and the servants promise not to tell Mr. Roosevelt. For a few weeks, he wore a cap so his father would not see the injury and begin to worry.

## ▶ On His Own

Most of Franklin's cousins and his wealthy neighbors had private tutors. Most of the boys left home to attend boarding school when they were twelve years old, but not Franklin. His mother could not bear the thought of being without her only child. He stayed home for two more years. It was not until he was fourteen that he finally left the mansion for Groton, a boarding school in Massachusetts. It was a "prep school," designed to prepare wealthy young men for college.

Not surprisingly, Franklin was not a very popular student at Groton. He earned respectable grades, but he still was not comfortable being with people his own age.

James Roosevelt died when his son was seventeen. Following her husband's death, Mrs. Roosevelt focused all her attention on her teenage son. When Franklin graduated from Groton and enrolled at Harvard College, she moved to Boston, Massachusetts, so that she could be just a few miles away from him.

At Harvard, Franklin earned fairly good grades. By now, he got along better with people his own age. He participated in some sports, but spent much of his time writing for the *Crimson*, the school newspaper. Ironically, his excellent preparation at Groton enabled him to complete his studies for his bachelor of arts (B.A.) degree in

just three years (1900–03). He remained for a fourth year at Harvard, during which he served as the editor of the *Crimson*.

## Cousin Theodore

Franklin Roosevelt was also becoming better acquainted with the fascinating man he called "Cousin Theodore." By the time Franklin was at Harvard, his distant cousin, Theodore Roosevelt, was one of the most famous men in the country. He had become Vice President Roosevelt in January 1900. Earlier, he had served as a state legislator, civil service commissioner, assistant secretary of the Navy, and police commissioner of New York City. Cousin Theodore had also had many exciting adventures. He had spent years in the Dakota Territory as a rancher and a cowboy. During the Spanish-American War, he had led a cavalry regiment called the Rough Riders up San Juan Hill in Cuba.

Sara Roosevelt did not want her son to grow up to be like Cousin Theodore. She wanted Franklin to enjoy a quiet, dignified life back at the mansion in New York.

## Cousin Eleanor

Franklin Roosevelt was also beginning to spend time with another distant cousin. Eleanor Roosevelt was Theodore's niece. The first time she had met her handsome, distant cousin was probably when she was two. Franklin had given her horseback rides at a family reunion when he was only four.

Eleanor Roosevelt was not a happy young woman. She dearly loved her late father, an alcoholic who had died when she was young. Her mother made fun of her for being too serious and plain looking. Because her daughter reminded her of a little old lady, she called her "Granny." Sadly, her mother also died when Eleanor was very young.

Eleanor was shy, serious, and quiet. Franklin was loud, happy, and confident. They seemed like a strange couple. But Franklin told his mother, "Cousin Eleanor has a very good mind."[1] She also had a very good heart. Even though she was a wealthy, privileged young woman, she cared about those who did not have those advantages. She volunteered in a settlement house, teaching exercises and dances to poor children. Once when a student got sick, Eleanor and Franklin took her home. The girl's home was

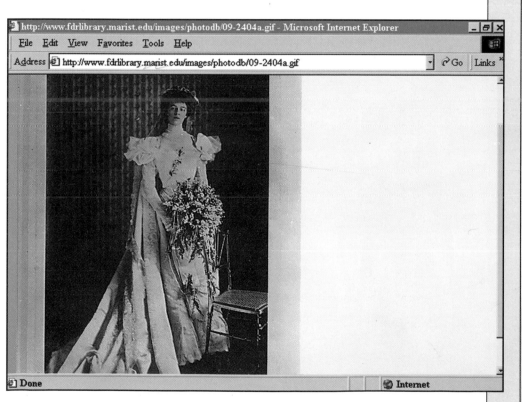

*Franklin intended to marry distant cousin Eleanor Roosevelt, despite his mother's objections. After failing to coax her son to change his mind, Sara accepted Eleanor as her son's choice. The couple was married on March 17, 1905.*

tiny, dark, and dirty. Franklin was shocked. "I didn't know people lived like that!" he said.[2]

When he was twenty-one and Eleanor was nineteen, Franklin Roosevelt asked her to marry him. Eleanor accepted. However, Sara Roosevelt thought the marriage was a terrible idea. She convinced her son that he was too young to be married. He agreed to postpone the wedding for a year. During that time, she hoped her son would forget his quiet sweetheart.

Sara Roosevelt tried to get Franklin a job in London, England, far from Eleanor. When that fell through, she took him on a long cruise through the Caribbean. After being away on the cruise, Franklin still wanted to marry Eleanor. He gave her an engagement ring on her twentieth birthday.

At the wedding, Eleanor's Uncle Theodore gave away the bride. By then Teddy Roosevelt was president of the United States. When the ceremony was over, he joked, "Well, Franklin, there's nothing like keeping the name in the family."[2] At the reception, the president was the center of attention. The guests wanted to hear his stories and laugh at his jokes. Nobody seemed to pay much attention to the newlyweds.

## ▶ A New Career

After graduation from Harvard, Franklin Roosevelt attended Columbia University Law School. He chose to take the New York state bar examination in the spring of 1907 and passed. He then quit

*Theodore Roosevelt, 1904.*

law school, never earning a degree. For three years he worked as a law clerk in New York City. During this time, he and Eleanor began raising their family—Anna, James, Elliott, Franklin, Jr., and John.

Working in a law office eventually bored Roosevelt. He did not want to spend the rest of his life looking up cases and writing legal briefs. Then in 1910, he got the opportunity he was looking for. Democratic leaders asked him to run for state senator from Hyde Park. The incumbent senator was a popular Republican, and would be tough to beat. Roosevelt did not care. He jumped at the chance to enter the race.

To get around the district, he rented a big red car, which he covered with flags. He spent a month meeting voters and giving speeches, usually with Eleanor at his side. During the campaign, he fell off a streetcar, badly skinning his elbows and knees. For a day, Eleanor nursed him back to health, soaking his wounds in disinfectant. Soon, he was back to work.

Roosevelt's speeches were not very good. He spoke too slowly and left long pauses between his sentences. On the plus side, Franklin Roosevelt was a handsome, smiling, energetic campaigner. The voters liked what they saw. Even though most of the voters in his district were Republicans, he won by 1,140 votes. The political career of Franklin Roosevelt had begun.

**Chapter 3 ▶**

# Setbacks and Successes, 1913–1932

**D**uring the years he spent in the New York senate, Franklin Roosevelt became a hardworking, well-liked politician. He also became a much better speaker. He talked faster and began sprinkling his speeches with jokes.

## ▶ Early Ambitions

The young politician caught the attention of President Woodrow Wilson, who appointed him assistant secretary of the Navy. It was a great job for Roosevelt. He loved ships and everything having to do with the sea. He toured naval bases and shipbuilding yards. He also worked in Washington, D.C., to organize the growing U.S. Navy. "I get my fingers into everything and there's no law against it," he said.[1]

World events made the Navy more important than ever. In 1914, World War I broke out in Europe. Germany, Austria-Hungary, and the Ottoman Empire lined up against France, Great Britain, and Russia. While trying to stay out of the struggle, the United States prepared for war. In 1917, the Americans finally joined the fight, declaring war on Germany.

Roosevelt was busier than ever. As part of his job, he visited American servicemen and toured European battle-fields. When he left for Washington, he said, "It is hard for me to go back to a dull office job in Washington after having visited the lines where our boys are making history."[2]

In 1920, Roosevelt was the Democratic vice presidential nominee. Here he campaigns in Dayton, Ohio, with presidential candidate James Cox (left) on the day Cox accepted the nomination.

The war ended in 1918 with an American victory. By then, Roosevelt was well known throughout the nation. In 1920, Democrats nominated him for vice president. He and James Cox, the presidential candidate, ran against the Republican team of Warren G. Harding and Calvin Coolidge.

Once again Roosevelt was a great campaigner. He made hundreds of speeches across the nation, but they could not get enough support. Harding was elected president in a landslide. Roosevelt was disappointed, but he was confident there were other important jobs in his future.

## A Frightening Diagnosis

The next summer, the Roosevelt family vacationed at their summer home on Campobello Island in Canada. The

children thought their father was a lot of fun. Anna said he was "a wonderful playmate who took long walks with you, sailed with you, could out-jump you and do a lot of things."[3]

On August 10, the family spotted a forest fire from their boat. Roosevelt led them ashore where they slapped at the flames with pine boughs. They rinsed off the smoke with a dip in the chilly water then jogged home.

Roosevelt was so tired he did not even change his clothing. Still wearing his wet swimsuit, he read his mail and the newspapers. By supper time, his body ached and shook with chills. He went to bed early. The next morning

The Roosevelt family spent many summers at their summer home on Campobello Island in Canada. It was here that Franklin suffered an attack of polio that ultimately changed the course of his life.

he was worse. His temperature reached 102 degrees. His left leg dragged when he tried to get up. Soon he could not move it at all. Before the day was over, his right leg would not move, either.

Eleanor was with her husband day and night trying to nurse him back to health. His fever broke, but he still could not use his legs. For a while, it was hard to move his hands and arms. Slowly he and his doctors came to the realization that he had polio.

It was a frightening diagnosis. Polio, or infantile paralysis, as it was known then, was a painful, mysterious disease that damaged nerves and left many of its victims paralyzed. In 1921, there was no vaccine to prevent polio or medicine to cure it. Roosevelt and his family hoped that he might recover. His goal was to walk again. For months, he exercised to improve his condition. He regained the use of his hands and arms, but his legs withered. He would never stand or walk again without assistance.

## ▷ Not Giving Up

Roosevelt's mother, Sara, argued that it was time for Franklin to retire to Hyde Park and take it easy for the rest of his life. His wife, Eleanor, thought that was a terrible idea. Maybe his legs did not work, but his brain was fine, and there was still a great deal he could accomplish.

Franklin listened to Eleanor. While he exercised to regain as much strength as he could, Eleanor traveled throughout New York gathering information for her husband. Even though she was still a very shy person, she made speech after speech to remind people that her husband was still around and concerned about public affairs.

Meanwhile, Roosevelt refused to feel sorry for himself. Once, while resting in a hospital bed, he punched a visitor in the chest. The poor man almost fell down. Roosevelt laughed. He wanted everybody to know there was still a lot of life left inside his tired body.

For the rest of his life, Roosevelt wore heavy metal braces under his pants to help him stand. When he was not in public, he used a wheelchair. When he had to move, he held on to big, strong men and swung his body by moving his shoulders. It looked like he was walking. It was an act. Roosevelt did not want any sympathy or pity. In public, he almost never mentioned his disability. Even after he became one of the most famous men in the world, hardly anyone knew that he could no longer walk.

Although he did not talk about it, that did not mean Roosevelt had not been changed by polio. Eleanor believed she understood the difference. "Anyone who has gone through great suffering," she said, "is bound to have a greater sympathy and understanding of the problems of mankind."[4]

## ▶ Therapy in Warm Springs

Roosevelt's most effective therapy came in Warm Springs, Georgia. The naturally heated waters helped ease the pain he still felt in his legs. They also allowed him to be comfortable while swimming. It was great exercise for him.

Many other polio patients also came to Warm Springs. Some could not afford the treatment. To help them, Roosevelt bought the springs and the land surrounding them. He established the Warm Springs Foundation, which provided treatment to thousands of polio sufferers.

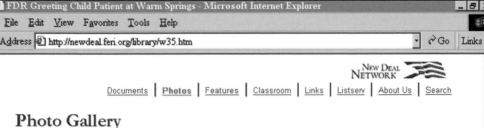

FDR Greeting Child Patient at Warm Springs - Microsoft Internet Explorer    _ 🗗 ✕

File   Edit   View   Favorites   Tools   Help

Address 🔊 http://newdeal.feri.org/library/w35.htm          ▾   ⌐Go   Links »

NEW DEAL
NETWORK

Documents | **Photos** | Features | Classroom | Links | Listserv | About Us | Search

## Photo Gallery

[ New Search ]

### FDR Greeting Child Patient at Warm Springs

**Location** : Warm Springs, GA
**Date** : 1930
**Agency** : PWA
**Owner** : FDRL
**Medium** : B&W Photo
**Control Number** : Photographs (FDR): c. 1930

Enlarged Image

**Listed Under:**
[Health Care][Therapeutic Centers][Warm Springs, GA]
[Issues and Events][Roosevelt and his Administration][Warm Springs, Georgia]

                                                          🌐 Internet

▲ *After purchasing the Warms Springs Resort in Georgia, Roosevelt formed the Warm Springs Foundation to help thousands of unprivileged polio patients receive treatment.*

## ▶ Back to Politics

By 1924, Roosevelt was healthy enough to attend the Democratic National Convention. His big smile and booming voice helped his listeners forget the awkward way he had to approach the podium. He made one of the convention's most important speeches. Now Franklin Roosevelt was back in the national spotlight.

Four years later, he gave the nominating speech for New York Governor Al Smith at the 1928 Democratic National Convention. Smith, the "happy warrior," was

selected to run against Herbert Hoover, the Republican candidate. After the convention, Roosevelt hoped to return to Warm Springs for more treatments. Smith, though, had other ideas. Since Smith was running for president, the party in New York needed somebody else to run for governor. Smith wanted Roosevelt. After a good deal of hesitation, Franklin finally agreed. Back in New York, he was nominated and, with Eleanor at his side, began a rigorous campaign.

Once again the Republicans won the White House in a landslide. Smith did not even win his home state of New York. Still, Roosevelt was a winner. In a very close election, he was elected governor in 1928.

## A New Deal

Soon America was in the midst of the Great Depression. Millions lost their jobs. Thousands of banks closed their doors. To many people, it did not seem as if President Hoover and the national government were doing enough to help the jobless, hungry, and homeless. But in New York, Governor Roosevelt pushed through relief for the unemployed and pensions for senior citizens. In a country rapidly losing hope, FDR, as the newspaper headlines called him, seemed to be one of the few leaders who was trying to help the people.

As the months went by, the economic crisis worsened. Al Smith declared that he would once again

*Vice President John Nance Garner.*

run for president. This time, he promised, he would beat Hoover. But Smith's old friend, Franklin Roosevelt, had other ideas. He decided he would run for president himself. The Democrats chose FDR. Roosevelt chose John Nance Garner as his running mate.

At his party's convention, Roosevelt promised Americans a "New Deal." He would try the programs that had worked in New York for the entire country. He would do whatever it took to make things better.

Herbert Hoover did not have a chance. Most Americans wanted an active leader with new ideas to stop the Great Depression. In one of the biggest landslides in American history, Roosevelt buried Hoover in the November 1932 election.

The country had to wait to see what its new president would do. According to the Constitution, Roosevelt would not take office until March 4, 1933. In the meantime, conditions got even worse. For four months, the nation waited. Roosevelt could do nothing until he made it into the White House.

He almost did not make it. After giving a speech in Miami, Florida, on February 15, the president-elect was the target of an angry man with a gun. Several people were hit—but not Roosevelt. One of the wounded was Anton Cermak, the mayor of Chicago. "I'm glad it was me instead of you," Cermak told FDR.[5] Three weeks later, the mayor was dead, but Franklin Delano Roosevelt was president of the United States.

## Chapter 4 ▶ The New Deal and Early Presidency, 1933–1940

**O**n March 4, 1933, Franklin Delano Roosevelt was inaugurated as the thirty-second president of the United States. Even though he was a millionaire who lived in a mansion, he immediately focused his attention on the poor people who had been hit hardest by the Great Depression.

### ▶ A New Deal

The new president immediately called a special session of Congress. Roosevelt and his advisors began proposing dozens of new programs, collectively called the New Deal. Congress quickly passed almost all of them.

FEMA (Federal Emergency Relief Administration) set aside money to help the unemployed. The Civil Works Administration (CWA) and later the Works Progress Administration (WPA) created thousands of jobs constructing public buildings, streets, and parks. The Civilian Conservation Corps (CCC) employed thousands of young men planting trees and building flood-control projects. The Tennessee Valley Authority (TVA) brought electricity to thousands of rural families. The National Recovery Administration (NRA) encouraged stable prices and higher wages. The Federal Deposit Insurance Corporation (FDIC) stabilized the banking system and guaranteed deposits.

One of Roosevelt's most important ideas was Social Security. For years, millions of older Americans could not afford to retire. Without a paycheck, they would not have

Tools    Search    Notes    Discuss                                    Go!

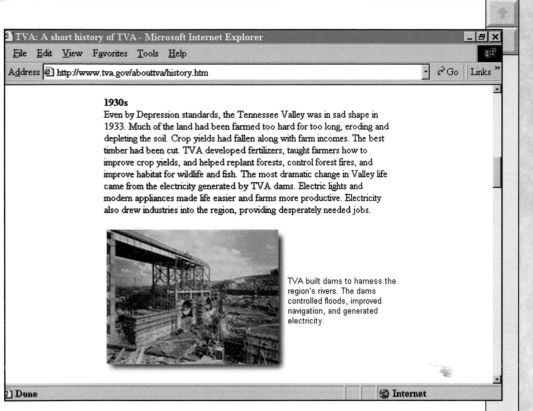

**1930s**
Even by Depression standards, the Tennessee Valley was in sad shape in 1933. Much of the land had been farmed too hard for too long, eroding and depleting the soil. Crop yields had fallen along with farm incomes. The best timber had been cut. TVA developed fertilizers, taught farmers how to improve crop yields, and helped replant forests, control forest fires, and improve habitat for wildlife and fish. The most dramatic change in Valley life came from the electricity generated by TVA dams. Electric lights and modern appliances made life easier and farms more productive. Electricity also drew industries into the region, providing desperately needed jobs.

TVA built dams to harness the region's rivers. The dams controlled floods, improved navigation, and generated electricity.

▲ *One of Roosevelt's programs, the Tennessee Valley Authority, improved communication and navigation, and provided electricity to people living in rural areas.*

enough to live on. Old age was a frightening prospect. Social Security changed all that. Under the program, a small portion of each worker's paycheck was saved toward his or her retirement. The government would match the workers' contribution. By the time of retirement, there would be enough money saved to guarantee a regular monthly check, called a pension.

Not everybody liked Roosevelt's programs. Some people believed he was having the government do too much for its citizens. They thought people should be responsible for taking care of themselves. They reflected

more conservative attitudes like former presidents Calvin Coolidge and Herbert Hoover.

## Trouble With the Supreme Court

Many wealthy Americans thought Roosevelt was poking his nose into their business. In its efforts to try to better working conditions, the National Recovery Administration was responsible for hundreds of new regulations. Some rich folks felt that if people were smart enough and worked hard enough, they should be able to run their companies any way they saw fit.

Critics made fun of the jobs created by the New Deal. They said millions of dollars were being spent on the CCC so that lazy people could get paid for raking a few leaves.

Roosevelt ignored his political opponents or laughed them off. Yet he could not ignore his most serious critics— the nine justices of the Supreme Court. According to the U.S. Constitution, the Supreme Court had the final say on all laws passed by Congress. The judges took a long, hard look at the New Deal legislation, and they did not like much of it.

In May 1935, the Supreme Court decided that the NRA put too much power in the hands of regulators who had not been elected. That meant the administration violated the Constitution, and therefore had to cease operations. The court stopped the work of several New Deal agencies.

The president was furious. He knew that the justices did not like his policies or his programs. He was afraid they would declare more of his programs unconstitutional. Since justices serve for life, it looked as though FDR was stuck with them.

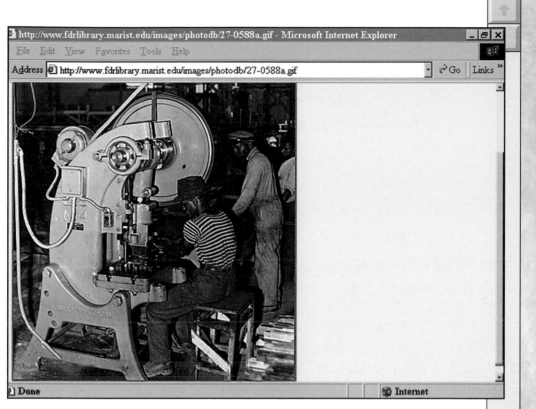

http://www.fdrlibrary.marist.edu/images/photodb/27-0588a.gif - Microsoft Internet Explorer

File  Edit  View  Favorites  Tools  Help

Address  http://www.fdrlibrary.marist.edu/images/photodb/27-0588a.gif        Go  Links

Done                                                                Internet

▲ *Although many criticized Roosevelt's government spending to create jobs, his programs provided factory jobs for many unemployed workers and increased the social morale.*

## ▶ "Happy Days Are Here Again"

The president still had the support of the great majority of the voters. His theme song was "Happy Days Are Here Again." Economic conditions were steadily improving and Roosevelt got much of the credit.

To build up support for his policies, the president worked hard to stay in touch with the people. As soon as he was inaugurated, he began a series of "fireside chats." These were brief talks given to the nation over the radio.

In the 1930s, Americans did not yet have televisions. Instead they listened to programs, music, and news on the

radio. Roosevelt was the first president to regularly use the new technology. Instead of making long formal speeches, his "fireside chats" were friendly little talks. Americans listened to them and trusted their leader. It seemed like he was sitting in their living rooms next to the fireplace. The chats increased support for Roosevelt's programs. They also helped make him enormously popular.

In a 1935 press conference, he said he would "try to increase the security and the happiness of a larger number of people . . . to give them more of the good things of life . . . to give them assurance that they are not going to starve in their old age."[1] Roosevelt knew how to use the media to get his message to the people.

## ▶ The Great Campaigners

Despite his handicap, FDR also traveled across the country giving speeches, visiting factories, and talking to leaders and citizens. When he toured a factory in Detroit, Michigan, one surprised worker yelled, "If it ain't old Frank!"[2] Roosevelt laughed and waved his hat at the man. He said that the mood of the nation had changed. The Americans he saw on his trips "were a hopeful people. They had courage written all over their faces. They looked cheerful."[3]

Still, it was Eleanor who did most of the traveling. When she returned to the White House, she spent hours giving reports of what she had seen to the president. She also shared her ideas on policies and programs with him. "They were a team," said their son, James.[4]

Mrs. Roosevelt was especially successful in helping win the support of African-American voters. She joined civil rights organizations and made many speeches backing equal rights for all races. African Americans, who had generally supported Republican Party candidates since the time of Abraham Lincoln, began turning to the Democratic Party.

By the 1936 presidential election, FDR had won the support of 71 percent of African-American voters. Most other voters backed him, too. He carried forty-six of the forty-eight states. That gave him an electoral vote margin of 523 to 6 over Alfred M. Landon, the governor of Kansas. Except for the unanimous election of George Washington, the 1936 election is the most one-sided landslide in American history.

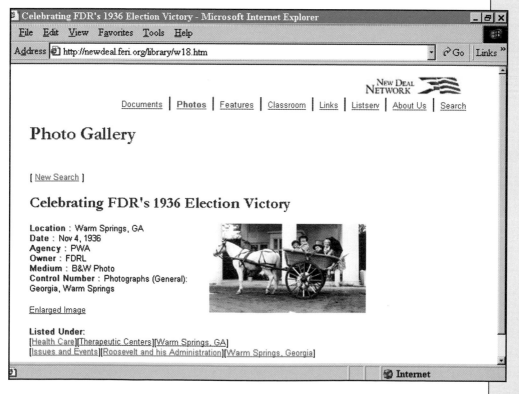

The Roosevelt family celebrates as FDR is elected to a third term as president.

## ▶ Court Packing Plan

FDR lost a major political fight in 1937, the first since he was elected. To get around the issue of lifetime appointment of the Supreme Court justices, Roosevelt turned to Congress for support. He wanted a law stating that every Supreme Court justice would be asked to retire within six months after turning seventy. If the justice chose to stay on the court, the president could appoint a new justice. Even the president's friends thought his Supreme Court idea was too extreme. He got little support for his plan to pack the court with justices he liked.

For their part, the justices stopped their attack on Roosevelt's policies. They allowed most of his latter programs to operate. The new agencies and regulations improved working conditions for millions of Americans. For the first time, most employees were guaranteed a minimum wage. Hours were limited and workers received extra pay for overtime. Child labor was almost totally eliminated.

Roosevelt won re-election again in 1940, becoming the only man to run for a third term as president. This time he beat Wendell Willkie with thirty-eight states and a 449–82 majority in the electoral college. Garner, who had served as vice president from 1933–41, opted to run for president in the 1940 election but lost the Democratic nomination to FDR. Henry Agard Wallace served as Roosevelt's vice president from 1941–45.

Economic conditions had improved and the United States was steadily shaking off the effects of the Great Depression, but all was not well in 1940. World War II was spreading across Europe, Africa, and Asia. Roosevelt worried that the United States would soon be dragged into the terrible war.

## Chapter 5 ▶

# World War II to the End, 1940–1945

**T**here were tensions throughout the world in the 1930s. Three countries: Japan, Germany, and Italy, had begun to expand their borders by taking territory from other countries.

### ▶ Preparing for War

In 1931, Japan took over Manchuria, a part of China. This led to a war between the Japanese and the Chinese. Italy invaded the African country of Ethiopia in 1935. By 1938, Japan controlled most of eastern China.

Without a war, Germany took Austria in 1938. The next year, Germans occupied Czechoslovakia and invaded Poland.

France and Great Britain declared war on Germany. The Japanese, Italians, and Germans joined together in an alliance that became known as the Axis powers. After France fell, Great Britain stood alone.

President Roosevelt worried that if Great Britain, too, was defeated, then it was just a matter of time before the Axis powers turned their might against the United States. Like Roosevelt, the sympathy of most Americans was with Great Britain. Unlike Germany, Japan, and Italy, Great Britain was a democracy, which had not invaded its neighbors.

While they were sympathetic to the British, there was very little interest among the American people in the United States becoming actively involved in the war. Most Americans took the attitude: Let them fight; it is not *our* problem.

The American Expericence/FDR/Propaganda Poster - Microsoft Internet Explorer

File   Edit   View   Favorites   Tools   Help

Address  http://www.pbs.org/wgbh/amex/presidents/nf/resource/fdr/primdocs/waste.html     Go   Links

Presidents                                    AMERICAN
                                              EXPERIENCE

WASTE HELPS THE ENEMY

CONSERVE MATERIAL

Waste Helps the Enemy

Intro | Presidential Record | In Their Own Words | Featured Presidents

Internet

▲ *A World War II propaganda poster emphasizes the importance of conservation of natural resources to the American public.*

Roosevelt, though, wanted the British to win, and he wanted the United States to be ready to fight if the time came. He negotiated an agreement with Winston Churchill, the British prime minister. In return for several naval bases in the Atlantic, the Americans gave Great Britain fifty old American destroyers. Roosevelt convinced Congress to let him send war supplies to the British.

FDR and Churchill signed the Atlantic Charter. Both countries promised not to take the territory of other nations. They agreed to respect free trade, freedom of the seas, and the right of all people to choose their own governments.

Roosevelt was also able to convince Congress to authorize the first peacetime draft in American history. The United States armed forces slowly began to grow.

## The United States Enters the War

The Axis nations made two serious mistakes in 1941. First, Germany invaded the Union of Soviet Socialist Republics (the U.S.S.R., or the Soviet Union). Then, Japan launched a surprise attack on the American naval base at Pearl Harbor, Hawaii. Suddenly, the Axis nations faced two new powerful enemies.

Roosevelt called December 7, the day of the Japanese attack, "a date which will live in infamy."[1] He pledged that the United States would fight on to total victory. The country united behind him.

Over the next few years, Roosevelt and Churchill worked closely to defeat Germany, Japan, and Italy. Along with Joseph Stalin, the leader of the U.S.S.R., they were known as the "Big Three." Together they planned the strategy that turned the tide of the war. Roosevelt

*...we here highly resolve that these dead shall not have died in vain...*

*REMEMBER DEC. 7th!*

On December 7, 1941, "a date which will live in infamy," Japanese planes attacked Pearl Harbor. This propaganda poster encourages the American public to remember Pearl Harbor Day.

▲ Pictured from left to right: Joseph Stalin, Theodore Roosevelt, and Winston Churchill were known as the "Big Three." Together, they planned a strategy that changed the tide of the war.

nicknamed Great Britain, the United States, and the U.S.S.R., the "United Nations," but they were usually called the Allies. Through this alliance, Roosevelt became the first American president to engage in diplomatic relations with the Soviet Union.

Within a year, United States and British troops were landing in Africa. Then, efforts in the Pacific were mounted slowly, but steadily, against the Japanese, checking their advance east and southeast. The battles of the Coral Sea (May 4–8) and Midway (June 4–6) in 1942, and the campaign to secure the Solomon Islands (from August 1942 until February 1943) were three of many such efforts. Italy surrendered in 1943.

## A Fourth Term

By 1944, Franklin Roosevelt was a tired old man. The burdens of his job and his physical problems had worn him out. Still, he did not want to leave office until he felt his job was done. "If the people command me to continue in this office and in this war," he said he would stay in the White House.[2] In November, the people made their decision and it was another landslide. Roosevelt defeated New York Governor Thomas E. Dewey, 432 electoral votes to 99. Roosevelt remains the only president to have been elected to office four times. Harry S Truman became Roosevelt's third vice president.

On June 6, 1944, Allied forces under American Gen. Dwight D. Eisenhower landed in Normandy, France, in what became known as the D-Day invasion. This was a decisive battle for the war in Europe. The allies secured a beachhead from which they could liberate France and Belgium and eventually defeat Nazi Germany.

Early in 1945, the frail president made a fourteen thousand-mile round trip to meet with Churchill and Stalin at Yalta in the Crimea (today known as the Ukraine). Together they planned the closing stages of the war.

When he returned to Washington, Roosevelt was too tired to stand for a speech to Congress. Instead he was wheeled into the Capitol building. "I hope you will pardon me," he said, "[but] it makes it a lot easier for me in not having to carry about ten pounds of steel around the bottom of my legs."[3] It was the first, and only, time he ever mentioned his braces in public.

## A New Dream

Before being wheeled out of the Capitol for the last time, FDR told the congressmen and senators about his dream

http://www.fdrlibrary.marist.edu/images/photodb/fdr300.gif - Microsoft Internet Explorer

File　Edit　View　Favorites　Tools　Help

Address　http://www.fdrlibrary.marist.edu/images/photodb/fdr300.gif　　Go　Links

Done　　Internet

*Although Roosevelt suffered a terrible battle as a result of polio, he never sought pity from the public. In fact, he did not mention his braces in public until 1945.*

for a permanent peacetime United Nations organization. Instead of fighting, nations would meet together and talk to settle their differences. He said they owed it to the American fighting men to make sure there would be no more terrible wars.

Then Roosevelt took a train to Warm Springs, where he could soak up the warm Georgia sun and relax. He told Vice President Harry Truman he would be feeling fine again soon.

On April 12, 1945, he planned to attend an afternoon barbecue. First, however, he needed to look over a few papers. Suddenly he tipped over and whispered, "I have a terrific pain in the back of my head."[4] It was a cerebral hemorrhage. A blood vessel in his brain had burst, and within a few hours he was dead.

Vice President Truman was sworn in as president. "There have been few men in all history the equal of the man into whose shoes I am stepping," he said. "I pray God I can measure up to the task."[5]

Less than two months after Roosevelt's death, Germany surrendered. On September 2, 1945, World War II ended when Japan surrendered. By then the peacetime United Nations had been organized. One of America's first delegates to the U.N. General Assembly was the president's widow, Eleanor Roosevelt. She was elected chairman of the Human Rights Commission and helped write the United Nations' Declaration of Human Rights. She died in 1962. Together Franklin and Eleanor Roosevelt were buried in the rose garden next to their mansion in Hyde Park, New York.

Franklin Roosevelt's presidency changed the United States. When he became president in 1933, the country was in crisis. When he died, the United States was the richest, most powerful nation on Earth.

Roosevelt was the first president Americans felt they knew personally. Because of his regular radio broadcasts, everyone knew the sound of his voice. Most of them supported him, electing him four times. In the two centuries since George Washington became the first president, nobody has served longer than FDR, and no one ever will. Six years after his death, Congress passed the Twenty-second Amendment to the Constitution. Presidents from that time forward have been limited to two terms in office.

▲ *This is the grave of Franklin and Eleanor Roosevelt. They are buried in a rose garden next to their mansion in Hyde Park, New York.*

Roosevelt's leadership brought Americans through the Great Depression and almost all of World War II. His policies changed the way the United States federal government worked. Dozens of new federal agencies were established to protect the rights of citizens, and to restrict the activities of business. Some people thought he made government too big and too powerful. Others, like most workers and people of minority groups, strongly supported him.

## Chapter Notes

### Chapter 1. "Nothing to Fear," 1932

1. William Manchester, *Glory and the Dream: A Narrative History of America 1932–1972* (New York: Bantam Books, 1988), p. 41.

2. Ibid.

3. Joseph Alsop, *FDR: A Centenary Remembrance* (New York: Viking Press, 1982), p. 85.

4. Manchester, p. 49.

5. "Inaugural Speech of Franklin Delano Roosevelt," *The Challenge of Democracy*, n.d., <http://www.hpol.org/fdr/inaug/> (June 19, 2001).

6. Manchester, p. 80.

7. Ibid., p. 82.

### Chapter 2. Early Life, 1880–1910

1. Joseph P. Lash, *Eleanor and Franklin* (New York: W. W. Norton & Company, Inc., 1971), p. 101.

2. Ibid., p. 135.

3. Ibid., p. 141.

### Chapter 3. Setbacks and Successes, 1913–1932

1. Joseph Alsop, *FDR: A Centenary Remembrance* (New York: Viking Press, 1982), p. 50.

2. Ibid., p. 53.

3. Doris Kearns Goodwin, *No Ordinary Time: Franklin and Eleanor Roosevelt: The Home Front in World War II* (New York: Simon & Schuster, 1994), p. 16.

4. Ibid., p. 17.

5. Alsop, p. 91.

### Chapter 4. The New Deal and Early Presidency, 1933–1940

1. Joseph Alsop, *FDR: A Centenary Remembrance* (New York: Viking Press, 1982), p. 161.

2. Doris Kearns Goodwin, *No Ordinary Time: Franklin and Eleanor Roosevelt: The Home Front in World War II* (New York: Simon & Schuster, 1994), p. 363.

3. Alsop, p. 136.

4. Ibid., p. 166.

**Chapter 5. World War II to the End, 1940–1945**

1. Joseph Alsop, *FDR: A Centenary Remembrance* (New York: Viking Press, 1982), p. 213.

2. Alsop, p. 225.

3. Ibid., p. 230.

4. Doris Kearns Goodwin, *No Ordinary Time: Franklin and Eleanor Roosevelt: The Home Front in World War II* (New York: Simon & Schuster, 1994), p. 602.

5. David McCullough, *Truman* (New York: Simon & Schuster, 1992), p. 352.

## Further Reading

Burns, James MacGregor. *Roosevelt: The Lion and the Fox.* San Diego, Calif.: Harcourt Trade Publishers, 1984.

Fremon, David K. *The Great Depression in American History.* Springfield, N.J.: Enslow Publishers, 1997.

Joseph, Paul. *Franklin D. Roosevelt.* Edina, Minn.: ABDO Publishing Company, 2000.

Lindop, Edmund. *Woodrow Wilson, Franklin D. Roosevelt, Harry S. Truman.* New York: Twenty-first Century Books, Inc., 1995.

Nardo, Don. *Franklin D. Roosevelt.* New York: Chelsea House Publishers, 1995.

Spies, Karen Bornemann. *Franklin D. Roosevelt.* Springfield, N.J.: Enslow Publishers, 1999.

Stein, R. Conrad. *World War II in Europe: America Goes to War.* Hillside, N.J.: Enslow Publishers, 1994.

————. *World War II in the Pacific: Remember Pearl Harbor.* Hillside, N.J.: Enslow Publishers, 1994.

Woog, Adam. *Roosevelt & the New Deal.* San Diego, Calif.: Lucent Books, 1997.

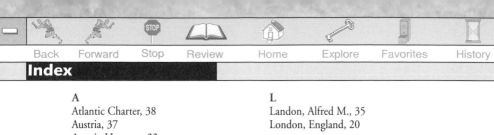
## Index

**A**
Atlantic Charter, 38
Austria, 37
Austria-Hungary, 22

**B**
"Big Three," 39

**C**
Cermak, Anton, 29
China, 37
Churchill, Winston, 38, 39, 41
Civil Works Administration, 30
Civilian Conservation Corps, 30, 32
Columbia University Law School, 20
Congress, 32, 36, 41
Coolidge, Calvin, 23, 32
Coral Sea, Battle of the, 40
Cox, James, 23
*Crimson*, 17–18
Czechoslovakia, 37

**D**
D-Day Invasion, 41
Declaration of Human Rights, 44
Democratic National Convention, 27
Dewey, Thomas E., 41

**E**
Eisenhower, Dwight D., 41

**F**
Federal Deposit Insurance Corporation,
    30
Federal Emergency Relief Administration,
    30
"fireside chats," 33–34, 44
France, 22, 37, 41

**G**
Garner, John Nance, 29, 36
Germany, 22, 37, 39, 41
Great Britain, 22, 37, 38, 40
Great Depression, 11–13, 28, 29, 30,
    36, 44
Groton, 17

**H**
Harding, Warren G., 23
Harvard College, 17, 18, 20
Hoover, Herbert, 12–13, 28, 29, 32
Human Rights Commission, 43
Hyde Park, New York, 14, 21, 25, 44

**I**
Italy, 37, 39, 40

**J**
Japan, 37, 39, 43

**L**
Landon, Alfred M., 35
London, England, 20

**M**
Midway, Battle of, 40

**N**
National Recovery Administration, 30, 32
New Deal, 13, 29, 30, 32
New York, 18, 21, 22, 25, 28, 29
Normandy, France, 41

**P**
Pearl Harbor, Hawaii, 39
Poland, 37
polio, 25, 26

**R**
Roosevelt, Anna, 21, 24
Roosevelt, Eleanor, 18–20, 21, 25, 26, 28,
    34, 43–44
Roosevelt, Elliott, 21
Roosevelt, Franklin, Jr., 21
Roosevelt, James (father), 14–15, 17
Roosevelt, James (son), 21, 34
Roosevelt, John, 21
Roosevelt, Sara, 15, 17, 18, 20, 25
Roosevelt, Theodore, 18, 20
Rough Riders, 18
Russia, 22

**S**
San Juan Hill, 18
Smith, Al, 27–28
Social Security, 30–31
Solomon Islands, 40
Soviet Union, 39–40
Spanish-American War, 18
Stalin, Joseph, 39, 41

**T**
Tennessee Valley Authority, 30
Truman, Harry S, 41, 42–43

**U**
United Nations, 40, 42–43

**W**
Wallace, Henry Agard, 36
Warm Springs, Georgia, 26, 28, 42
Willkie, Wendell, 36
Wilson, Woodrow, 22
Works Progress Administration, 30
World War I, 22
World War II, 36, 43–44

**Y**
Yalta Conference, 41